'HE SP

obin's

drama

m

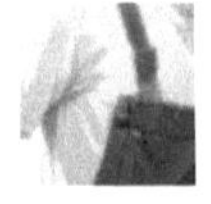

new di

m und

that, Ro

ɔ take l

ou also

.dler fe

rks”

not so

at, I'm (

s impo

, and st

her noc

bout th

'rayers

estless

an So

said, "

od also

ıs and (

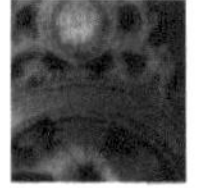

he Spir

d him,

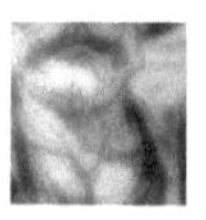

n bring

"You

tacting

qualif

:o the I

1 to tun

ie conv

; howe

: comfo

ıd shoı

which

(Org

l Dime

n you h

erior? D

are de

t he a

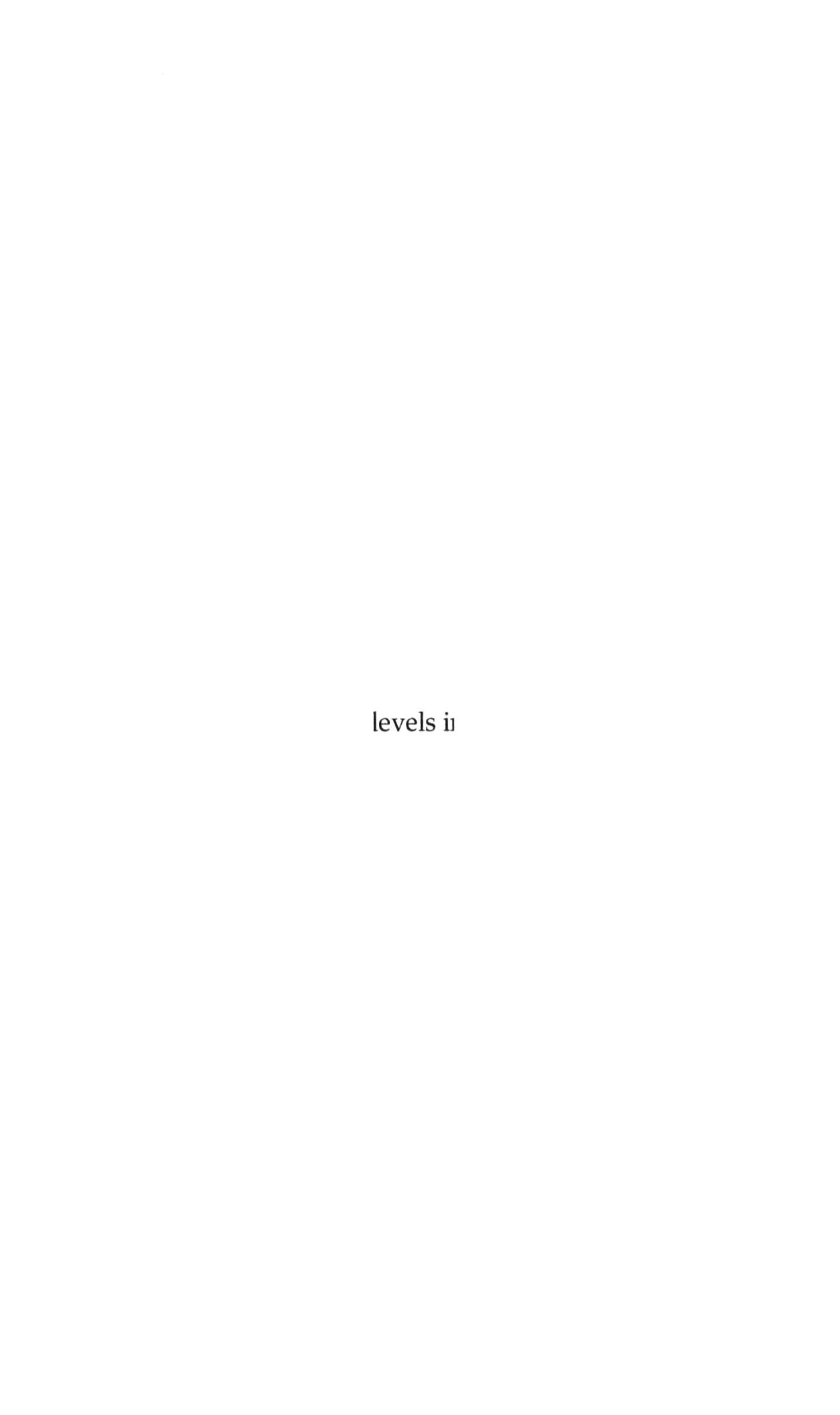
levels i

nd gair

progra

of conf

Ego can

ions th

y pray

also for

inclusi

ild rela

n any f

ed on t

both p

bavoid

echnol

nan wit